"A Voteless People Is A Hopeless People"

A Book Of Quotations

60 YEARS ANNIVERSARY
Commemoration Edition

Selma to Montgomery Alabama March
AMELIA BOYNTON ROBINSON
MOTHER OF THE VOTING RIGHTS MOVEMENT

By Ronnie K Barnes

Illustrator: Obayomi Israel olamide

Amelia Book of Quotes copyright @ 2025 by The Weaver Company. All Rights Reserved.

This book of quotations has historical nonfiction facts, with direct quotes from Amelia Boynton Robinson, known as the "Matriarch of the Voting Rights Movement." This book of quotes gives a narrative of Amelia Boynton Robinson's lifetime of quotes, which spanned over nine decades. No parts of this book may be reproduced in any form or by any electronic or mechanical means including storage and retrieval systems, without permission in writing from the author. The only exception is by a reviewer, who may quote shorts in a review.

This is a book of exact quotes from Amelia is a work of nonfiction characters. Names, characters, places and incidents either are products of the author's research of real and true events or some names, if mentioned, may be imaginary names or fictitious to protect the identity of the person involved. Any resemblance to actual persons, living or dead, events, or locales are true to its entirety and not coincidental.

Legal Disclaimer. This book is based, in part, upon actual events, persons, voting and civil rights organizations. No part of this publication may be reproduced in whole or in part, or stored in a retrieval system, or transmitted in any form or by any means, electronic, mechanical, photocopying, recording, or otherwise, without written permission of the publisher.

ISBN: 978-1-7354442-5-3

Illustrator: Obayomi Israel Olamide

Ronnie K Barnes: visit my website at Ronniethewriterweaver.com
RKBarnes0824@gmail.com
RKBarnes0824@hotmail.com

Printed in the United States of America First Printing January 2025

BRIDGING THE GAP FOR THE NEXT GENERATIONS

"We Shall Overcome"

AMELIA BOYNTON ROBINSON
A BOOK OF QUOTES

Words of Wisdom and Inspirations
"Queen Mother"

Notes

Boynton Robinson fought for civil rights and voting rights for black people. She was brutally beaten for helping to lead a 1965 civil rights march which became known today as "Bloody Sunday." Amelia Boynton and Samuel William "S.W." Boynton married in the 1930s. Her birthplace is Savannah, Georgiathe in August 18, 1905. She graduated from Tuskegee Institute with a home economics degree before further pursuing her education at Tennessee State University, Virginia State University and Temple University.

Amelia Boynton early in life would become the co-founder of the Dallas County Voters League in 1933; and she would move on to hold African American voter registration drives in Selma from the 1930s through 1950s.met while working as agricultural extension agents in Selma, Alabama. Their partnership was not only personal but also professional, as they both worked tirelessly to encourage Black people to register to vote and buy land. Ameia Boynton Robinson was a civil rights pioneer who led voting rights for black people,

In1964, Amelia Boynton Robinson ran on the Democratic ticket for a seat in Congress from Alabama-becoming the first African American woman to do so, as well as the first woman to run as a Democratic candidate for Congress in Alabama. Although she didn't win her seat, Boynton earned 10 percent of the vote.

It would be Amelia who would ask Dr. King and the Southern Christian Leadership Conference to come to Selma and help promote the cause. According to research and studies, King eagerly accepted. Soon after, King and the SCLC set up their headquarters at Boynton's home. There, they planned the Selma to Montgomery March of March 7, 1965.

A newspaper photo of Boynton lying bloody and beaten brought attention to the cause. Bloody Sunday prompted President Lyndon B. Johnson to sign the Voting Rights Act on August 6, 1965; Amelia would be invited to attend the landmark event as guest of honor.

Boynton Robinson was introduced to the LaRouche Movement in 1983, she became a board member and then vice-chairperson of the Schiller Institute. The Schiller Institute was founded to defend the rights of all humanity. The Schiller Institute published her book Bridges over Jordan in 1992. Also, in 1992, Boynton Robinson co-founded the International Civil Rights Solidarity Movement, where she received worldwide recognition for her service to humanity. In 1990 Boynton Robinson was awarded the Martin Luther King Jr. Foundation Medal of Freedom: In 2003 she was awarded the National Visionary Leadership Award, and in 2005, Boynton Robison and her husband S.W. Boynton were honored on the Fortieth Anniversary of Bloody Sunday in Selma.

Boynton Robinson spent the latter part of her career touring the nation and speaking worldwide on behalf of the Schiller Institute to promote civil and human rights.

Amelia Boynton Robinson passed away on August 28, 2015.

I can never do justice to the great feeling of amazement and encouragement I felt when perhaps for the first time in American History, white citizens of a Southern state banded together to come to Selma and show their indignation about the injustices against the African Americans.

Amelia Boynton Robinson

I was born to Lead

It's important that young people know about the struggles we faced to get to the point we are today. Only then will they appreciate the hard-won freedom of blacks in this country.

Amelia Boynton Robinson

I wasn't looking for notoriety when we marched. But if that's what it took to get attention, I didn't care how many licks I got. It just made me even more determined to fight for our cause.

Amelia Boynton Robinson

When we got a little across the bridge, I saw these state troopers; I saw the sheriff's deputies—some of them were on the Selma side. I saw the police. And the state troopers were in front. And I said to my friend Marie Foster, My gosh! These people look like tin soldiers.

Amelia Boynton Robinson

There were screams, cries, groans, and moans as the people were brutally beaten from the front of the line all the way back to the church—a distance of more than a mile. State troopers and the sheriff and his men beat and clubbed to the ground almost everyone on the march.

Amelia Boynton Robinson

Strangely enough, this freedom or privilege was purchased by people of all races who gave themselves: Blood, sweat, tears, as well as death, paying the supreme price for freedom. There are unsung heroes and heroines whom we will never know.

Amelia Boynton Robinson

I was brutally beaten unconscious during the march in Selma Alabama. I was beaten by an Alabama state trooper while attempting to cross the Edmund Pettus Bridge. This first march became known as [Bloody Sunday].

Amelia Boynton Robinson

Edmund Pettus Bridge, a bridge crossing the Alabama River in Selma, Alabama. This site became known as "Bloody Sunday," a landmark event in the history of the American Civil Rights Movement. On that day, March 7, 1965, white law-enforcement officers violently dispersed protesters, the vast majority of whom were African Americans, as they crossed the bridge during the first attempt to initiate the Selma March.

Politics, History

You see, many people paid the supreme price, for people to register and to vote. My husband died because of his trying to get people to register, and freeing them off of these plantations. Jimmy Lee Jackson died, because he attended the meeting and wanted to know more about how to help to register and get these people through that.[1]

Amelia Boynton Robinson

As long as we were helping them to improve their homes that was my job, and the county agent helping them to produce more cattle, produce more crops and better crops, oh it was great; they thought a whole lot of us. But as soon as they found out that these good farmers who were doing the producing that they were leaving their farms where they had nobody, because they didn't know anything about farming then problems, threats, and harassment started to happen for me and my husband and myself.[2]

Amelia Boynton Robinson

[1] Schiller Institute. Winning the Right To Vote The Battle for Selma https//archive.schillerinstitute.com/books/amelia_excerpt.html. The Schiller Institute, January 19, 2004. URL.
[2] Schiller Institute. Winning the Right To Vote The Battle for Selma https//archive.schillerinstitute.com/books/amelia_excerpt.html. The Schiller Institute, January 19, 2004. URL.

And we were getting them off of the farm. And these were the things that made [the white power structure] hate us so badly. We were helping these people to get places that they could buy. And I don't care how evil some people are, the evil seemingly is a forerunner, and you can see the evil more than you can see the good. There was a white guy, who had a store in the city of Selma. And he sold farm products, like plows and whatnot. Well, he told my husband, "Boynton, if any of your people can find any kind of property, any kind of farm, and want to leave the farm that they're on, I will loan them money free of interest for the first year." And he did. And many of them left the farm.[3]

Amelia Boynton Robinson

[3] Ibid

A Voteless People is a Hopeless People.

Amelia Boynton Robinson

I lived to look back and evaluate the accomplishment from the struggle and set a timetable for the distance we have to go. Selma, Alabama, can be the candle of hope that will shine all over the world: as the light of justice, compassion, and love is exchanged for castle prods, tear gas, billy clubs, and attack dogs.

Amelia Boynton Robinson

Part of the line being across the bridge, we found ourselves less than 50 yards from the human wall. The commander of the troops, on a sound truck, spoke through a bullhorn and commanded us to "stop where you are." Hosea Williams of SCLC and Cong. John Lewis and all the line behind them halted. Hosea said, "May I say something?" Major Cloud retorted, "No, you may not. Charge on them, men."[4]

Amelia Boynton Robinson

[4] Ibid

The African-Americans standing in line were indignant, but the only consolation they could give me was, "Go on to jail, Mrs. Boynton, you'll not be alone. We will be with you." What more consolation would one need? With a final grand push, the sheriff shoved me into a deputy's car and said, "Arrest her and put her in jail."[5]

Amelia Boynton Robinson

[5] Ibid

I was then brutally handled, pushed down the hall, and thrown into a jail cell. Later, from the cell, I heard the group, who had cheered me on at the courthouse. They had been marched the three blocks to the jail, singing, "Oh freedom, oh freedom, oh freedom over me. And before I'll be a slave, I'll be buried in my grave, and go home to my Lord and be free." This song had never sounded so sweet to me as when they stood before the barred door that led to the jail itself and began to sing again.[6]

Amelia Boynton Robinson

[6] Ibid

Your vote is your ticket to First Class Citizenship... Use It!

Amelia Boynton Robinson

TAKE BACK YOUR MIND

When you get what you want in the struggle of life,
And the world calls you King-For-A-Day,
Then, go to the mirror and look at yourself,
And see what that guy has to say.

It's never a man's mother or father or son,
Your mistakes are – NOT USING YOUR BRAIN.
It is only yourself, and nobody else,
You're the one whom you have to blame.

Just face the mirror and look at yourself
Do you really like what you see?
A guy who could be the greatest of men,
But you traded for NO LIBERTY.

Look good at the guy staring back at you,
Whose life was as bright as the sun.
Did you know as a pawn you'd find yourself,
When you thought it was all fun?

Take a look at yourself before it's too late.
Straighten up and act real fast.
You still have a chance to mend your ways,
If you are true to the guy in the glass.

Poem by Amelia Boynton Robinson

Poem By Author

My Grey Hairs
My Grey Hairs on my Body tells a story.
My Grey Hairs Signifies youth and the prime of my life.
My Grey Hairs tells a story of pain and suffering and
not so happy feelings of a Black man at times.
My Grey Hairs. Yes, My Grey Hairs.
My Grey Hairs looks like salt and pepper in an
hourglass
My Grey Hairs tells a story.
It whispers, Father time.

Ronnie Barnes

www.ingramcontent.com/pod-product-compliance
Lightning Source LLC
Chambersburg PA
CBHW080627170426
43209CB00007B/1529